Are you looking to effortlessly transition away from foods that create illness, zap your energy and age you way beyond your years? Fantastic!

Chef Tina Jo is introducing her 7 Day Juice Feasting Program for those of you who want to make a change but don't know how to! What's Juice Feasting you ask? Simply put, Juice Feasting is consuming hearty, abundant, fresh raw juices! There's No fasting here, folks, only feasting upon the best that nature offers ...

FRESH RAW DELICIOUS ORGANIC FRUIT AND VEGETABLE JUICES!

I began my journey to a raw vegan diet back in 1999 while searching for relief from some serious health problems. A friend suggested trying a raw vegan detox program. Skeptical as I was, I decided to give it a try. Not only did it work for me, it was life changing. It has been quite a journey, but as they say, the rest is history!

The transition to a raw lifestyle was pretty easy for me; I felt better than I had in years and I wanted more than anything to NOT EVER go back to the "old me." However, I would occasionally find myself making poor food choices out of sheer boredom with my recipe repertoire. I eventually made my way to the halls of the Living Light Culinary Arts Institute in northern California where I learned how to recreate the fun I used to have in the kitchen as a child; but this time, creating fabulous raw vegan meals. I became so impassioned with my new skills that I just had to share them and thus "Chef Tina Jo" was born! It started with a facebook page, than a website and lots of hard work; before I knew it we had our own show and were part of the FMG network with over 100,000 daily viewers. Next came our show on a local cable television station, our second website was born and I was authoring my book series.

My friends and family began noticing marked improvements in my energy levels, mood, and appearance. Upon seeing my transformation, some even decided to join me in the raw lifestyle and my journey into coaching literally unfolded before me.

I can honestly say that it was DIVINE INSPIRATION that set the idea of the 7 Day Juice Feast directly in front of me!

Juice feasting would begin to clean out the body while building it up at the same time. Whether they craved salty, sweet, spicy, or bitter, I could come up with a concoction that worked for each of my loved ones. Juicing could incorporate all the flavors of the Standard American Diet that they had become accustomed into a raw diet. I pitched the idea and they loved it! This book was born out of the experiences of these kind souls who became my first group of feasters. They had a blast experimenting with their juicers and coming up with their own unique recipes which they could hardly wait to share with the group.The support that developed among my first group of feasters proved to be an iron pillar that not only got them through some tough times during their juice feast but eventually helped ALL of them make the transition to a predominately raw diet.

So now, I would like to share my 7 Day Juice, All Juice, Nothing but the Juice Feast with you. Whether you are looking to shed a few pounds, give your body a good cleanse, or make the transition to a raw lifestyle, this book will help get you on your way. I wrote it to help you make the transition to a healthier you! You're that important to me! You've got nothing to lose (except the things you WANT to lose) and a whole lot to gain! What are you waiting for? Read on, my friends, and welcome to the amazing world of raw!

MEDICAL DISCLAIMER

This book is not intended to be or provide medical advice. All the content, including text, graphics, images and information is for general information and educational purposes only. It is not intended to be a substitute for professional treatment or diagnosis. The author and publisher of this book are not responsible for any adverse effects that may occur from the application of the information in this book. You are encouraged to make your own healthcare decisions based on your own research and in partnership with a qualified healthcare professional.

INSTRUCTIONS

I highly recommend that you get yourself cozy and read the entire book before getting started. This process will ensure that you get yourself in theright frame of mind to begin your feast.

TABLE OF CONTENTS

TABLE OF CONTENTS

I first came to raw vegan food out of sheer desperation. I was battling health problems and a friend suggested I try a raw vegan detox program. Honestly, I was skeptical. But my western doctor was steering me towards a hysterectomy, so I decided to give the detox route a try. I figured that at the very least, eating fruits and vegetables for thirty days had to be healthy and would help me shed a few pounds.

I went into the program without a thought about raw vegan eating as a lifestyle. It just seemed so extreme to live on fruit and salad. But then something amazing happened; I came away from the detox program feeling fantastic! I reached out to others who had turned to a raw vegan lifestyle to correct health ailments and every single person I talked to had only positive things to say. Maybe this wasn't so extreme, I told myself, and decided to continue the regimen at home.

My medical problems soon began to clear up and even my doctor changed his mind! He said surgery was no longer needed and I was hooked on the raw vegan lifestyle. I truly felt my best eating a raw diet and my clean bill of health just drove the point home.

Back in those early days I thought eating raw meant eating a whole lot of salads and cold foods, but I soon discovered how wrong I was. So, what does raw vegan food really mean? First off, raw vegan foods are whole plant foods such as organic fruits, vegetables, fresh herbs and leafy greens; then there are nuts and seeds, seaweeds and amazing wildcrafted superfoods, fermented foods and even sprouting. Raw vegan foods contain no animal products and have all their enzymes intact. You'll find no white flour, gluten, refined sugar, cholesterol or trans-fats in a raw foods diet. It is believed that cooking foods above 115 degrees Fahrenheit actually destroys vital nutrients and enzymes. In other words, raw does not mean cold.

WHAT ARE ENZYMES?

Enzymes are proteins that increase the rate of biochemical reactions in the body, including digestion. If you eat food with the naturally occurring enzymes intact, your digestive organs don't have to work as hard to break down and absorb your food. This frees up a tremendous amount of energy that your body can use to do more important things, like fight disease. There are three major enzymes involved in digestion: protease digests proteins, amylase digests starches, and lipase digests fats. These enzymes are present in perfect proportions in raw plant foods.

So what happens if you don't take in enough enzymes? Enzyme deficiencies have been linked to a host of health problems, including malabsorption of nutrients, allergic reactions, poor wound healing, skin problems (such as acne and eczema), premature aging, and degenerative disease.

Raw vegans enjoy pizza, lasagna, hearty soups and so much more. It's just not cooked or made in the traditional way. Blending and dehydrating are processes that heat foods without destroying enzymes and nutrients. Fermenting, sprouting, and food processing are other techniques raw vegans use to add more excitement and variety to meals.

In the meantime, if you are looking for a great introduction to some fabulous raw foods, I encourage you to visit ChefTinaJo.com and try out some of my recipes. I guarantee your taste buds will be pleasantly surprised by the incredibly mouthwatering taste of raw vegan foods. From comfort foods to desserts and gourmet meals for entertaining, you'll find it all. If you decide to take it a step further, there are books and coaching programs on ChefTinaJo.com to help you get started.

What have you got to lose? You wouldn't be here now if you weren't ready to take a positive step to a healthier lifestyle. It's all about the journey forward. So come on, let's take the next step to a whole new healthier you!

Here's what you'll get with my 7 day solid food vacation!!

• More energy, more vitality, and a clear mind

• A clearer understanding of what your body wants and needs

• A squeaky clean digestive tract

• Personal Support

• Reduction of sugar and salt cravings

• Weight loss

• 'Revved up' metabolism

SECTION 1
INTRODUCTION

INTRODUCTION

CONGRATULATIONS! I AM THRILLED THAT YOU HAVE MADE THE DECISION TO EMBARK ON THIS AMAZING SOLID FOOD VACATION WITH ME!

This program is all about you. Remember that! It's important to start that mindset now. There's nothing wrong with taking care of yourself, making time for yourself and putting yourself first! This program is more than just learning how to put amazing food into your body. It's also about learning how to love and really care for yourself; how to take time and nurture yourself. Most of us are so busy working, running from appointment to appointment and taking care of others, that we have forgotten (or have never learned) how to really nurture ourselves. Well that's all about to change! The next 10 days are going to be all about you; your vacation from food cravings, body bloat and bad self-talk. You can do this! It's only 7 days and I'm right here with you!

This 7 Day Juice Feasting Program will start healing your body from the inside out with your very first delectable mouthful! My 7 Day All Juice (Nothing but the Juice) Feast will cleanse your intestinal tract, eliminating years of undigested food, toxins, and putrefied poisons leaving you feeling renewed, rejuvenated, and perhaps more alive than you've ever felt before! You'll not only experience more energy in the next 7 days, but I'll give you tips on making quick and delicious juices that will get the whole family in on the act! We'll cover equipment, recipes and the mind body spirit connection. You don't need to worry about a thing! You will have my support and guidance throughout the entire journey.

> Not a fast, not denial, not abstaining — this is all about indulging, feasting, and enjoying your food! You're going to learn ways to pamper yourself, love yourself and get comfortable with your body.

FEASTING VS. FASTING, INDULGE IN THE DIFFERENCE

My 7 Day Juice Feast is different from "FASTING" programs because it is designed to provide your body with superior nutrition without leaving you feeling depleted or deprived as fasting often does. Most people take in small amounts of food and calories when fasting causing the metabolism to slow and energy to plummet. Fasting makes it extremely difficult (or virtually impossible) to function and thrive in life as we know it.

INTRODUCTION

With today's busy lifestyles who has time for LESS energy? We need MORE energy and better health!

Most people are so used to feeling run down, tired, and sick that they have forgotten what it truly feels like to have great health and an abundance of energy! Feasting teaches your body to receive, absorb, and assimilate an abundance of unadulterated pure delicious nutrition. It's about empowerment and abundance; NOT SACRIFICE OR ABSTINENCE! Yes! That means you can and should have as much as you want! When's the last time you heard that and it didn't add five pounds to your hips? Now get ready because we are about to really speed up your metabolism as we load your body with some amazing nutrients!

WHY RAW FOOD? BE KIND TO YOUR BODY AND IT WILL BE KIND TO YOU!

For 7 days you will be feasting on some of the healthiest foods on the planet — raw foods.

A raw food diet is a diet based on unprocessed and uncooked whole live foods, such as fresh fruits and vegetables, sprouts, seeds, nuts, grains, beans, dried fruit, and seaweed. Although this list may seem limited or boring to some, I can assure you it is far from that! One of my passions is teaching others that raw vegan foods don't have to be boring. There's so much more to life then eating carrot sticks, salads and fruit plates!

Raw food is defined as unprocessed raw vegan foods (absolutely no animal products) that have not been heated above **115 degrees Fahrenheit**. Heating food above 115 degrees Fahrenheit destroys the enzymes that assist in digestion and absorption of food, thus diminishing optimal nutritional value. A diet consisting of at least 80% whole raw live foods provides optimum health. My 7 Day Juice Feast will give you an idea of just how vibrant and alive a raw diet makes a body feel! Are you starting to get curious and excited?

If you are not familiar with my fabulous recipes, you've really got something to look forward to! I've included a section with some of my favorite smoothies to help you transition back to solid food after your feast!

Years of stress, poor food choices and inferior food quality greatly impair the digestive tract, limiting the body's ability to absorb and assimilate micro nutrients. Juicing pre-digests your food, helping your body to absorb most of the plentiful nutrients your food has to offer. Juice feasting cleanses the body while supplying an abundance of essential vitamins, minerals and enzymes and delivering powerful antioxidants to virtually every cell in the body! It's like power-washing every cell, literally cleansing your body from the inside out.

Each day of the 7 Day Juice Feast includes a minimum of 4 quarts (1 gallon!) of delicious freshly squeezed juice with nutrient-packed LIVE RAW ORGANIC green veggies and fruits. (This does not include your intake of water, herbal teas and coconut water.) It takes about 15 pounds of food to make one gallon of juice! It's important to consume this amount for optimal health and energy. Less than this will cause your metabolism to slow and your energy to slump as we discussed previously in regards to fasting. This is something you definitely want to prevent. Remember, this is all about abundance, energy and thriving! SO DRINK UP!

> You are about to embark on an amazing journey, healing your body from the inside out!

BENEFITS OF FEASTING: FEEL THE DIFFERENCE!

During this feast your digestion will become easier and faster.

Juicing removes the fiber from your food which allows your body to assimilate the nutrients from the juice quickly. Because your body easily absorbs these nutrients, it uses the saved energy to go on to other things like healing your body. You will start to notice that your bowel movements will become easier and more frequent. Your body will really start to cleanse matter from the small intestine and colon; you may even notice mucus in your stools. This is completely normal and a welcomed sign; it means your body is working towards optimal health. Celebrate!! It is estimated that the average person can have between 4–25 pounds of this "built-up" intestinal matter in their colon and it can just keep accumulating over the years! This stuff is toxic, so get ready to say bye, bye to toxicity and extra pounds and hello to healthy intestines!

This is more nutrition than your body has ever received — unless you were nursed as a baby — and how long ago was that?

Juicers separate juice from fiber providing your body with instant access to the vitamins, nutrients and live enzymes in your food. Smoothies merely blend up the fiber essentially preventing release of the absorption of key nutrients.

"The intestines can store a vast amount of this partially digested, putrefying matter," claims natural health expert, Richard Anderson, N.D., N.M.D. "Some intestines, when autopsied, have weighed up to 40 pounds and were distended to a diameter of 12 inches with only a pencil-thin channel through which the feces could move. That 40 pounds was due to caked layers of encrusted mucus, mixed with fecal matter, bizarrely resembling hardened blackish-green truck tire rubber or an old piece of dried rawhide."

Sorry to be so graphic, but it's important to know what is inside many of our bodies!

Juicers separate juice from fiber providing your body with instant access to the vitamins, nutrients and live enzymes in your food. Smoothies merely blend up the fiber, essentially preventing release of the absorption of key nutrients.

JUICING VS. SMOOTHIES: IT'S ALL ABOUT THE FIBER

Juicing allows your body to conserve massive amounts of energy normally diverted to digestive processes. When the fiber is removed, nutrients and vitamins are assimilated immediately, providing your cells with instant nourishment. When the digestive organs don't have to work as hard that energy can be used to regenerate, replenish, and heal tissues and cells leaving you feeling vibrant and renewed!

But I always thought fiber was good for me!!

Yes, fiber is good for you! Insoluble fiber moves bulk through your intestines acting like little brooms sweeping away excess debris from the intestinal walls. Soluble fiber binds with fatty acids and moves them out of the bloodstream. It also slows stomach emptying time thus slowing down the release and absorption of sugars. In the days before the Juice Feast, I advise you to eat a plethora of raw fruits and veggies (with all the fiber intact) starting today in order to prepare your body for the cleansing and replenishing that my 7 Day Juice Feast provides. Remember, Juice Feasting is about getting an ABUNDANCE of pure unadulterated goodness into all of your cells and fiber interferes with that process. You can absolutely have smoothies when you are finished feasting.

HERE'S WHAT THE EXPERTS HAVE TO SAY ...

"Juice Feasting is a very effective way to help people regain their health and lose weight over a safe extended period of time while still maintaining their work, family and worldly responsibilities." — Dr. Gabriel Cousins

"Juicing fresh fruits & vegetables is a great way to get the vital nutrients you need." — Dr. Mehmet Oz

"I am firmly convinced that juicing is the final key to giving you radiant, energetic life, and truly optimal health" and "I think juicing is phenomenal!" — Dr. Joseph Mercola

SECTION 3
PREPARING YOUR INNER AND OUTER SPACE

PREPARING YOUR INNER AND OUTER SPACE

As with all my coaching programs, I am going to make this feast easy and fun. Your daily meals will be ready to eat in as little as 90 seconds. All you have to do is push your food into your juicer and watch it transform into pure liquid sunshine right before your eyes. Preparing your meals couldn't get much simpler than this!

We will begin with a 5 day preparation period to get you physically, mentally, and spiritually ready for your juice feast.

I like to recommend that you start with cleaning out your kitchen. Not only should you get rid of all temptations lurking in the refrigerator and pantry, but get rid of any clutter that might have accumulated on tables or counter space. Starting with an uncluttered living space rejuvenates me almost as much as my juice feasts!

I suggest going through the entire house and getting rid of things that have outworn their usefulness. You will be amazed how clearing out your living space will help you clear out your mind. This really works! Don't get overwhelmed by this process; get excited! Change is a-comin'!

Switch things up a bit, move things around, rearrange the furniture! This makes everything feel new and clearer, just like your body will be feeling in the very near future!

Start some healthy habits now!

MAKE A PLACE AND TIME FOR MEDITATION

I like to use the term RPM. It means rise, pee, meditate! I found that mediating first thing in the morning improves the likelihood that, well, I'll meditate! It doesn't have to be for hours or even half an hour. Try 15 minutes a day. Allow that for yourself. If need be, set the alarm clock ahead 15 minutes so this can fit into your schedule. The most important thing is not to try too hard.

Don't make this a big deal. Meditating is the easiest thing that our minds can do; perhaps that is why it is so powerful. If you don't have a meditation technique this is a good time to find one. If silent meditation does not appeal to you, try yoga, Tai Chi, praying, or just sitting or walking in nature paying close attention to the natural world around you and giving thanks.

PREPARING YOUR INNER AND OUTER SPACE

PAMPER YOURSELF

This preparation period and your feasting week should absolutely involve some pampering and indulgence. Take a few long luxurious soaks in the tub reading a book or listening to music that inspires you. Treat yourself to a massage. Get an acupuncture treatment. Whatever it is you decide to do, do it for you. Do something that you've always wanted to do or something that you haven't done in a long time. Last year on one of my feasts, I learned how to body board! It was invigorating, great exercise and I overcame my fear of the water. Whatever you do, it doesn't have to be expensive or extreme; just be good to yourself. Be kind and loving. Appreciate your body, just as it is now and all it does for you. Remember; this is about you, so make time for yourself.

START MAKING HEALTHY FOOD CHOICES

Fill your uncluttered kitchen with fresh vegetables and fruits and start eating more of them than you ever have before. Now is a good time to stop eating meats, refined sugars and processed starches.

GET FIRED UP AND GET INSPIRED!

People just like you have been juicing to improve their health for decades. Imagine how you will feel when you have more stamina, more vitality and a happy, healthy body. Read testimonials of people who have changed their lives by juicing feasting. Start searching and you will find inspiring stories of juice feasters all over the world, including stories of folks overcoming diseases like cancer and diabetes with nothing but juice. I am not a doctor and cannot possibly advise you on juicing as medicine, but there are people out there who claim that juicing saved their lives. If consuming live raw juices can positively affect an ill person's health so dramatically, imagine what it will do for you!

PROUDLY PLACE YOUR JUICER IN A PROMINENT PLACE ...

... on the countertop and start using it. Place a cutting board by your juicer. Keep your knives in a handy, yet safe, spot. Keep a blank notepad in the same location; this is really handy when you're creating juices. It will help you to remember those juice recipes you LOVE and those that you don't want to repeat again. Experiment with juice recipes and become aware of what foods your body and taste buds like best. As you progress through these stages of preparation, you may notice that you are already feeling better!

SECTION 4
LET'S GO SHOPPING!

The first thing you will need is a shopping list! Simply print, then check the ingredients you'd like to incorporate and start shopping!

VEGETABLES	FRUIT	OTHER ITEMS *
Celery	Green apples	Young coconuts or boxed coconut juice
Kale	Oranges	Hemp oil
Carrots	Strawberries	Coconut oil
Cucumbers	Lemons	Garlic
Tomatoes	Limes	Stevia
Spinach	Grapes	Raw honey
Sprouts	Pears	Flaxseed (ground)
Cabbage	Tangelos	Celtic Sea Salt
WheatGrass	Peaches	Himalayan Pink Salt
Beets (including the greens)	Nectarines	Mint
Yams	Cranberries	Ginger Root
Romaine Lettuce	Cantaloupe	Basil
Collard Greens	Honeydew	Parsley
Arugula	Watermelon	Cilantro
Red Bell Pepper	Plums	Black peppercorns
Swiss Chard	Pineapple	Dill
Orange Bell Pepper	Fuji Apples	Thyme
Dandelion Greens	Blueberries	Oregano
	Blackberries	Rosemary

- **Coconut juice** is nature's sport drink. It is loaded with electrolytes which will help keep you hydrated as your body begins to purge itself.
- **Raw honey or Stevia** can make some juices more palatable.
- **Himalayan Pink or Sea salt** provides the salty flavor while providing dozens of trace minerals.
- **Herbs** add extra nutrition and flavor while spicing your juice up!
- **Wide mouth mason jars,** I recommend these for many reasons. They can be purchased in quart size, which makes it super easy to track your daily intake, they are glass so no worries about nasty plastic contaminates and they are easy to clean! The wide mouth will allow your hand and a sponge to enter for easy clean up.

ADDITIONAL SUPPLEMENTS

Additional supplements you might want to pick up:

- **Digestive enzymes** help to speed up digestion and act as a mini-cleanse on an empty belly. Sunfood's Beauty Enzymes are my personal favorite. *http://cheftinajo.com/r/enzymes*
- **Wheat grass, barley grass and/or spirulina green powders** are nutrient-dense additions that help to alkalize the body. *http://cheftinajo.com/r/wheatgrass*
- **Bee pollen granules** sweeten up life and are a complete food containing more minerals than I can count. *http://cheftinajo.com/r/beepollen*
- **Dulse flakes and kelp granules** add a bit of saltiness and are loaded with minerals, as are all sea vegetables. *http://cheftinajo.com/r/kelp*
- **Fenugreek** helps the body rid itself of mucus.

Be aware that specific nutritional deficiencies are common on a prolonged juice feast. Be prepared by stocking up on the following as taking them while you are feasting will be beneficial:

- **Calcium:** Calcium citrate is the best absorbed supplement. Be sure "USP" is on the label. This ensures that the product contains elemental calcium which is the only calcium the intestines can actually absorb.
- **A liquid Iron supplement:** "Floradix Iron + Herbs" is my absolute favorite! It is a plant-based elixir packed with elemental iron and other nutrients which promote intestinal absorption.
- **Sublingual Vitamin B12:** Be sure to purchase B 12 that includes a B-Complex as the B vitamins work synergistically. Taking one B vitamin without the others actually works against you.
- **Folate (Folic Acid):** The US RDA for folate is 400 micrograms per day. If your B 12 tablet does not have adequate supply of folate, be sure to supplement.

Caloric Deficiencies are often a concern with a detox, fast, and cleanse — but remember folks, we are feasting!

Have as many juicy snacks as you feel you need. Please don't ever deprive yourself! And by all means, make sure you are getting enough. A number of factors must be considered to calculate an individuals recommended daily caloric intake; including gender, age group, and activity levels. The average moderately active woman should consume about 2000 calories a day while the average moderately active man should consume about 2500.

You can find more specific information here: *http://www.webmd.com/diet/features/estimated-calorie-requirement*

Find out if you are getting what you need here: *http://www.nutritiondata.com*

BUY OR GROW ORGANIC!

If you aren't growing your own, buy local and organic as much as possible!! I know that initially it costs a little more, but you are worth it! Think about how much being sick costs you! There is so much information out there about the dangers of conventionally grown and genetically modified foods. Buying locally is your best bet to ensure superior quality and freshness. Check out your local Farmers' Markets to find good fresh whole organic food, rather than buying at the supermarket.

I suggest that you initially purchase enough produce to get you through the first few days of juice feasting. This will help you get into the swing of things.

Or better yet, grow your own! You don't have to have the land or even a green thumb to become part of My Organic Acres! This is like nothing you've ever seen before! You will lease and have access to your own 240/120 square foot Organic Garden 24/7 from the comfort of your own living room through the magic of the computer. You will tell your own personal gardener what favorite fruits and vegetables you wish to plant and they'll get started. Can you imagine fresh whole organic food that is affordable all year round? Well dream no more, it's now a reality! The only thing you will miss is that pungent compost odor that wafts through your garden.

You will have an expert gardener assigned to till, plant, hoe, and harvest your crops for you. You can then choose to sell all or a portion of your crops in an on-line farmers market, have all or a portion of your crops shipped direct to your house for dinner, or give all or a portion of your crops to feed the hungry! All of this will be handled for you by the expert staff at Organic Acres. Come join me and thousands of others at My Organic Acres. *http://ChefTinaJo.com/r/MyOrganicAcres*

My Organic Acres pledges to use 100% USDA certified organic seeds, soil, and fertilizer and all of your crops will be guaranteed. You can know exactly where your food comes from!

SECTION 5:
LET THE
FEASTING BEGIN!

LET THE FEASTING BEGIN!

THE 1/4 GREEN RULE

When preparing your juices for the first few days, a good rule of thumb is to use 1 part green vegetables to 3 parts other veggies, like carrot, apple, beet etc. This sweeter base combination makes the drink far more palatable. The last thing I want is you to be totally turned off by a bitter tasting juice. I also suggest that you try to keep it simple by limiting the number of ingredients to 4 or 5 per juice. The more you add, the more complex the

flavors and the more likely you'll have a bitter juice. Additionally, too many ingredients tend to cause a bit of bloating. So keep things simple and stick to the 1/4 Green Rule.

Consult my recommended shopping list and stick to The 1/4 Green Rule to get a better idea of what kind of juicy goodness most appeals to you.

> The 1/4 Green Rule: When preparing your juices for the first few days, a good rule of thumb is to use 1 part green vegetables to 3 parts other veggies, like carrot, apple, beet etc. The sweeter base combination makes the drink far more palatable.

If you are unsure, purchase 10 heads of lettuce, 4 large cucumbers, 4 heads of celery and pick up a variety of your favorite fruits and veggies to get you started. After a few days your comfort zone will widen and you will have a better idea of what your body and taste buds are craving. You'll feel more creative and ready to experiment by your next shopping trip.

WHAT TO JUICE

Just about anything that can be eaten raw can be juiced. **Isn't that exciting?** The possibilities are limitless!

There are more vitamins and nutrients in one day's worth of juicing than in an entire week of the Standard American Diet! Very soon your body will start asking for (and craving) these nutritious raw foods. These foods and nutrients are what your body needs most.

LET THE FEASTING BEGIN!

Add In Greens And Celery. Another thing to keep in mind when creating your juices is the importance of juicing 2 pounds of dark leafy greens and one head of celery per day. This may seem like a lot and if you were eating it rather than juicing, it would be! In fact, for many, it would be nearly impossible for most folks to consume this amount of fresh whole organic food! **Are you starting to see the benefits of juicing?**

Why dark leafy greens and celery? The greens help the body to become alkalized, mineralized and grounded. The celery is rich in minerals and organic sodium. Celery also contains 95% water, which helps keep the body hydrated. This makes these ingredients vital for your feast. Anything else you want to include in your raw juice menu is all up to you. This is where the fun begins!

Carrots are yummy, sweet, and packed with beta carotene. Don't overdo it, though — you can turn orange. Seriously! My friend's son drank carrot juice every morning when he was young and his skin literally turned orange. If this starts to happen to you, just lay off the carrots for a day or two and you will be fine. I mean ladies come on, can you imagine how hard it will be to coordinate your outfits?

Here's a great tip when shopping for carrots, ask your grocer for juicing carrots. They are far less expensive than regular carrots, they just aren't as pretty.

Beets are an excellent blood builder and are also sweet and delicious in juices! Remember that they will turn your stools red so don't be alarmed when this happens.

Cucumbers are a super food, packed with electrolytes and a variety of nutrients including calcium, iron, magnesium, phosphorous, potassium, zinc, and most of the B vitamins (but not B12, so don't forget the sublingual B12 tabs!)

Celery is tasty, nutritious, and will add a salty flavor. Juice the leaves too — that way you'll get all the healthy benefits celery has to offer.

Dark Leafy Greens such as spinach, chard, kale and a variety of lettuces are nutritional powerhouses! Leafy greens are among the most nutritious foods on the planet. Most contain a wealth of minerals including iron, calcium, potassium, and magnesium. They are packed with vitamins including vitamins C, E, K and many of the B vitamins. Dark leafy greens even have a touch of Omega-3. Make sure you get those greens into your juicy pleasures!

Cabbage is extremely healing to the intestines. Both the white and purple varieties will do wonders for restoring intestinal health. And it tastes great, really!

Tomatoes are loaded with vitamins A, C, and K, potassium, iron, and the antioxidant lycopene. Choose red ripe juicy varieties for the best taste and nutrition!

Apples and pears are incredibly hydrating. A medium sized apple has 10 mg of calcium while a pear has 9 mg. Apples are rich in potassium with 159 mg and pears are not far behind at 119 mg. Pears also contain many of the B vitamins.

Papayas are famous for their digestive enzymes but they are also an excellent source of vitamins A, C, and E, lutein, and lycopene.

Watermelon can help regulate blood sugar, is packed with vitamins and minerals and even contains Omega-6.

These are just a few examples of the amazing benefits of some of nature's whole live raw foods! It is by no means exhaustive!

MORE HEALTHY HABITS

Chew Your Juice!

One important element of juicing is to CHEW before you swallow. The chewing action releases saliva which stimulates digestive enzymes in your mouth. This will mix with your meal and enhance the digestive processes, helping you to better assimilate your food. **This means minimal belly aches (or none at all).**

Drink Lots of Water!

And when you think you've had enough, drink more! It is absolutely imperative that you begin each day with a large glass of PURIFIED water. Drinking a large glass of water in the morning (with a squeeze of lemon if you have it) is important because your body becomes dehydrated while you sleep and it needs to be replenished. Purified water is different from regular bottled water in that purified water passes through a sophisticated carbon block. With bottled water, you never really know what you are getting. However, most filters take out many of the minerals that are essential to get your water into your cells. Adding a pinch of sea salt (or, better yet, Himalayan pink salt) will provide your cells with instant access to your water. Here's a great link to some great products to improve your water: *http://ChefTinaJo.com/r/water*

Experts say to ensure you're getting your proper daily intake of water you can follow this simple formula. Take your body weight in pounds, divide in half, and drink that many ounces of water daily. You may count half of the liquid in your juices as water.

LET THE FEASTING BEGIN!

Get A Dry Brush!

Dry skin brushing sloughs off dead skin cells, leaving your skin with a radiant glow and it feels absolutely amazing! The stimulation also helps reduce cellulite, cleanses the lymphatic system, tightens the skin (preventing premature aging), stimulates circulation, removes dead skin layers, strengthens the immune system, improves the function of the nervous system, stimulates the oil-producing glands, tones the muscles, helps digestion and it's inexpensive, invigorating and EASY! All this from one little brush and 5 minutes of your time! **You can't go wrong!**

You can pick up a dry brush at almost any pharmacy, grocery store, or department store. Be sure to choose one with a back attachment. This will help you get at all those tricky spots. Here's my favorite: *http://ChefTinaJo.com/r/drybrush* — I dry brush standing in the in the shower, just before bathing or showering and follow with my favorite moisturizer which leaves me feeling silky smooth and rejuvenated as I go on with my day.

With dry brushing you always want to be moving towards your heart except over your belly. Start at your feet brushing upwards towards your heart. Once you're at your chest and shoulders brush down again moving towards your heart. Then brush down along your belly. It may take a bit to get the motion down, but once you do you'll be hooked!

Consider buying some essential oils and add them to your bath water to enhance relaxation as you detox *(http://ChefTinaJo.com/r/essentialoils)*. Lavender is incredibly calming and is especially helpful for those suffering from caffeine withdrawal headaches.

Keep Your Toothbrush And A Tongue Scraper Handy.

Your teeth and tongue may feel a bit fuzzy for the first few days. By keeping a tooth brush and tongue scraper on hand you can quickly eliminate both sensations. A tongue scraper also gets rid of excess bacteria in your mouth. Watch all the changes that start to happen on your tongue. It's amazing how every part of us if affected by what we eat. We just never stop long enough to think about it or really look at all the clues that our bodies give us. Paying attention to our bodies is the first step to living more consciously.

Clean Out Your Colon Via Colonic Irrigation Or Enemas.

As you read earlier, the average person eating the standard American diet can have between 4 and 40 pounds of metabolic waste sitting in their colons and adhering to its walls. The condition of our colon has a significant impact on every organ in our bodies and our overall wellbeing. Giving it a good cleaning now and then is soooo important; especially during your feast!

FOUR STEPS
TO SUCCESS!

1. KNOW WHAT MOTIVATES YOU!

The key to success whenever you are embarking on a new project is to know what motivates you. Find your unique motivation for doing my 7 Day Juice Feast. Ask yourself what is the most important reason you want to do this? Maybe all that toxic waste in your intestines is slowing you down. Maybe you want to shed those extra pounds hanging out around your belly to get into that bikini or look super sexy for your significant other. Maybe you have specific health issues that feasting will help alleviate or maybe you are sick and tired of feeling sick and tired! Or maybe you are just looking to improve your energy and vitality. Know what motivates you and remember it! This will help you get through this process and help you achieve your goal.

I want you to find the ONE most important reason you want to go on a solid food vacation and make that your daily mantra. Keep it running through your mind all the time! I put post-it notes all over the house to help keep me motivated - on the bathroom mirror, on the refrigerator, inside my cabinet doors, on the dashboard of the car... you get the idea. Give yourself constant reminders to help you stay motivated!

2. SET GOALS!

Setting small realistic goals will make the 7 Day Juice Feast a breeze. Don't look at 7 days as a mountain. I want you to take things one day at a time or, better yet, one juicy meal at a time and then the next and the next... Before you know it,

> **Tina Jo's Four Steps to Success**
> • Know what motivates you!
> • Set goals!
> • Surround yourself with support!
> • Prepare yourself properly!

your feast will be over and you will find that you want to continue filling your body with delicious healthy foods.

Imagine your body as your vehicle and filling it only with Grade A/Premium fuel because you want it to last as long as possible.

I want you to fantasize about your first juicy meal right now. Think about how delicious that first glass of pure unadulterated liquid sunshine will taste and feel and all the marvelous things it will do for your body. Imagine that the feast is over; how will you look? What will you be wearing? Where will you be? See yourself perhaps celebrating with friends, family or that special someone. Everyone is admiring your new look and congratulating you on a job well done. Now really feel what that's going to be like! Get excited about your new look, health and energy! Don't think I am crazy; it really works! This will help you get over the hump of the first few days when your body is withdrawing and you're changing your old eating patterns.

3. SURROUND YOURSELF WITH SUPPORT!

It is very easy to let goals slip by the wayside when you haven't got the emotional support you need.

Get your friends and family on board too! Let them know that you are planning to feast. I bet you will find at least one person who will be there for you through the ups and downs (if there are any downs) when you just need someone to listen. You may find that one of them may want to feast with you!

If you have kids, this is a great time to introduce them to what fresh whole organic juice tastes like! Have them help you come up with recipes. Make enough for them to enjoy with their meals while you feast on yours!

Kids love getting in on the act. As you cut the produce, allow your children to add the veggies and fruits to the juicer and watch them in delight as the juice is extracted. Kids love this! You're showing them a healthy lifestyle by leading by example. It's a win, win for everyone.

4. PREPARE YOURSELF PROPERLY.

Now is a great time to start preparing your body, mind and environment. To ensure success you absolutely should rid your home, your thoughts, and your life of all junk! That means junk food, meat, dairy, refined sugar, processed foods, clutter and bad self talk. Take back your kitchen and make it your sanctuary. Get the "junk" out of your house, mind and body and don't let it back in! Give any contraband food away, now! Donate it to a shelter or give to a neighbor. If you don't have it in the house you won't be tempted.

Now you are ready to stock up so go to My Organic Acres *http://ChefTinaJo.com/r/ MyOrganicAcres*, your local farmers' market or grocer and buy a rainbow of fruits and vegetables to get you going!

WHAT TO EXPECT WHEN YOU ARE FEASTING

WHAT TO EXPECT WHEN YOU ARE FEASTING

THE FIRST FEW DAYS ARE THE HARDEST

In all fairness, I am going to tell you that **the first 2 or 3 days of feasting are generally the hardest**, depending on your normal diet. It is normal to experience a bit of bloating, gas, and/or uneasiness in the first few days of the feast. Some people feel a bit tired. Some develop a minor headache.If you regularly indulge in fresh fruits and vegetables, the transition will be easier. In fact, you may experience no discomfort at all.

A juice a day will get you on your way. If your diet is lacking in fruits and greens, as suggested earlier, you should start preparing yourself now. Begin by eating at least 3 servings of fresh fruits and vegetables or at the very least drink one quart of fresh juice a day. It's a great way to start your day and the immediate results will amaze you! Then when you actually start your feast, your body will be already on board!

Drinking lots of water is another important factor to minimize discomfort. Maintaining proper hydration is especially helpful to prevent and relieve headaches. Drink all the water, coconut juice and decaffeinated tea you want; this will only ensure hydration.

Don't forget to breathe. I know — you wouldn't be alive if you weren't breathing, but are you breathing deeply? Breathing in through the nose and out through the mouth slowly and deeply will bring oxygen to all your cells relaxing and rejuvenating your entire body. My acupuncturist recommends doing this 10 times every morning before I get out of bed, again when I get into bed, and whenever I think of it in between. I have to tell you that when I remember to do it, I do feel fabulous!

WHAT COMES IN MUST COME OUT!

Bowel movements. You will start to notice that your bowel movements will become easier and more frequent. Your body is starting to cleanse matter from the intestines and the colon. You may also notice mucus in your stools. This is completely normal and a welcomed sign. It means your body is cleaning itself out. Naturally you will be urinating more. With more liquid going into your body, more will be coming out.

Other changes. You may experience an outbreak of acne, increased body odor, bad breath and a runny nose. These are toxins releasing through your skin and the other end of your digestive tract. Again, this is perfectly normal, it's a good sign and it will go away.

EXPECT TO FEEL BETTER THAN YOU HAVE IN A LONG TIME!

My hope is that after 7 days of feasting, you will feel so good that you will never want to go back to eating the Standard American Diet or, at the very least, you will continue to juice daily and eat more fruits and vegetables!

This may sound silly to you right now, but after the first week of nothing but fresh organic homemade juices, I had better focus and mental clarity. I felt more at harmony with everything around me. I felt more spiritual, more vibrant, more alive and I knew it was because of what I was putting into my body. I was learning to be one with the earth's delicious bounty. MY LIFE FORCE ENERGY WAS NEVER HIGHER and I was on top of the world. It was as if my brain suddenly turned on. I felt absolutely radiant and glowing and I know you will too! I hope you will join me on my 7 Day Juice Feast and experience the same thing or better.

SECTION 8:
RETURNING TO SOLID FOOD

RETURNING TO SOLID FOOD

You may find it more difficult to return to solid food after your juice feast than it was to begin it. Start by slowly introducing nutritious solid foods. You will most likely discover that your body really likes certain fruits and vegetables juiced more than others so those would be the best to start but in very small portions! You will find that your appetite is drastically smaller than it was prior to feasting because your stomach will shrink so don't give it more than it needs.

Introduce new foods slowly. Replace one juiced meal with one raw organic fruit or vegetable for the first day. Eat two raw meals on the second day and three raw meals on the third.

Be aware of how your body reacts as new foods are introduced, paying particular attention to any rise or fall in energy levels, digestion, and cravings and plan your next meals accordingly.

I suggest eating at least 75% fresh raw foods for the first 10 days after your feast. The other 25% should be whole grains such as brown rice, whole grain breads and pastas, cooked beans and vegetables. Definitely stay away from animal products at least for the first 10 days and, if you do eat them, remember to keep the portions very small.

A tip to remember is whenever eating cooked foods take replacement enzymes to help your body digest the food. *http://ChefTinaJo.com/r/enzymes*

Be sure to chew your food thoroughly which will break things down more completely making digestion easier on your stomach and intestines.

The new healthier you will probably find that you don't want to return to your old eating habits, so enjoy your new healthier lifestyle!

SECTION 9:
FREQUENTLY ASKED QUESTIONS

IS THE 7 DAY JUICE FEAST GOOD FOR EVERYONE?

Children and women who are pregnant or nursing need more dietary fat, protein, and fiber than most and should not partake in the juice feast due to their bodies' high nutritional demands.

People with anemia, low blood sugar, diabetes, eating disorders, kidney disease, liver disease, malnutrition, addictions, underweight, impaired immune function, low blood pressure, ulcerative colitis, cancer, terminal illness, epilepsy, other chronic conditions and elderly folks with weak constitutions (fatigue, diarrhea/loose stools, feeling cold all the time) should seek the advice of a trusted physician and may want to modify juice feasting to best meet their specific nutritional needs.

People who have recently undergone or will be undergoing surgical procedures should not feast!

WHAT IS THE DIFFERENCE BETWEEN A JUICE "FAST" AND A JUICE "FEAST"?

Juice Feasting differs from juice fasting because you, 'the feaster,' will get all the calories you are accustomed to. The only difference is the delivery system. This will insure that you meet the energy requirements needed to go about your normal daily routine without feeling tired and worn-out. We are going to speed up your metabolism and load your body with some amazing nutrients with my 7 Day Juice Feast. Juice fasts limit daily caloric intake which slows down metabolic functions, leaving fasters feeling worn out and depleted. Fasting just doesn't fit into a busy lifestyle, while feasting is ideal!

CAN I CONTINUE MY JUICE FEAST BEYOND THE 7 DAYS?

Absolutely! You may find that you enjoy the benefits of the 7 Day Juice Feast so much that you don't want to stop and you don't have too! Remember Juice Feasting provides your body with everything it needs to cleanse your system thoroughly and deeply without interfering with your life. Because all your caloric needs are being met, you can safely and easily juice for much longer than you could on a traditional fast, detox, or cleansing program.

THAT IS A LOT OF LIQUID. CAN MY BODY REALLY HANDLE THAT MUCH?

Unbelievably, the human body can take a lot of things we wouldn't dream possible. As a very petite person myself, I also had a few doubts about drinking so much liquid at one time, much less 4 times a day! But my body handled it very well. I was always full and satisfied. I found myself visiting the bathroom quite frequently but that is to be expected and welcomed as our bodies are flushing out excess waste.

CAN I MAKE 4 QUARTS IN THE MORNING AND STORE IT FOR THE REST OF THE DAY?

Making your juice fresh and drinking it ASAP will give you optimal results. Because juices are live foods, they oxidize quickly losing some enzymatic effectiveness as they sit around. Some natural occurring enzymes, vitamins and minerals are lost within 20 to 30 minutes of the juicing process. The longer it sits, the more nutrients are lost. However, if you are unable to freshly juice a meal due to your lifestyle I suggest freezing a quart to take with you. Although, it is not optimal, it is better than skipping a meal or interrupting your feast by eating solid food.

WHAT IF I PREFER MY JUICE COLD?

Keep your produce in the refrigerator and your juice will be cold or enjoy it over ice.

WHAT HAPPENS IF I GET HUNGRY BETWEEN JUICE MEALS?

You should juice whenever you feel hungry! Drinking lots of water, coconut juice and your favorite decaffeinated teas will fill your belly and help control hunger. You may also add some ground flax or green powder to your juices, this also helps to fill you up. Just remember you may not be feeling quite as full this week as you felt when you were consuming your Standard American Diet. I don't want you to feel full but I do what you to feel satisfied, so please do not deprive yourself. This is a feast, so if you're hungry have more and do so guilt free!

WHAT EQUIPMENT WILL I NEED?

Wide mouth quart mason jars, knives, cutting board and a good quality juicer. That's it!

Wide mouth jars make clean up a snap but any quart size jars will do, such as large tomato sauce or pickle jars. Mason jars can typically be purchased at any health food store or department store. A tip on juicers: If you don't already have a juicer I suggest that you buy the highest quality juicer that fits your budget. Not all juicers are created equal but there are some good ones out there for just about any budget. I use and highly recommend the Omega Juicer. *http://ChefTinaJo/r/juicer*

Don't be penny wise and pound foolish. Years ago when I started juicing, I thought I'd save myself some money and I purchased a less expensive juicer. What happened fairly quickly is that it broke down. I ran back out and purchased another one, then another, then another, until I finally broke down and purchased a high quality juicer. I've had my current juicer for years now, more years then I can remember.

The moral of the story, if I would have purchased the darn thing from the start, I would have saved myself a ton of money.

I'VE NEVER REALLY EATEN RAW FOODS OTHER THAN AN OCCASIONAL SALAD. AM I READY FOR THIS?

Absolutely! Remember, this is just a short introduction to one of the healthiest lifestyles on the planet, so there is nothing to worry about. Other than the few exceptions previously mentioned, just about everyone can start a juice feast.

WILL I NEED TO STAY CLOSE TO A BATHROOM FOR A WEEK?

No! You will be visiting the bathroom more than usual and this is a good thing. You should be having at least 3-4 bowel movements a day but not diarrhea. If you do develop severe or lasting diarrhea your body is telling you that now is not the time to be doing the juice feast.

CAN I MAKE MY OWN JUICE RECIPES?

Yes, of course! In fact, I encourage you to experiment with your own concoctions and learn what's best for you. Remember, listen to your body. You may find that certain fruits or veggies make you feel better than others. Just remember the 1/4 GREEN RULE and no more than 4- 5 ingredients in each juice.

WHAT ARE DIGESTIVE ENZYMES AND DO YOU RECOMMEND ANYTHING IN PARTICULAR?

Digestive enzymes help the body to reformulate foods consumed each day into usable by-products that nourish the various components located in cell structures, tissues, and every organ. I like Sunfood's Beauty Enzymes. *http://ChefTinaJo.com/r/enzymes*

ANY FRUITS OR VEGETABLES YOU RECOMMEND I DON'T USE?

Grapefruit juice should not be used during your juicy vacation. This is particularly important for people taking certain prescription drugs as a compound in the fruit can change the way certain prescription drugs are metabolized in the body. Recent studies suggest that this may also be true of pomegranate juice so I would err on the side of caution and avoid it if you take prescription medications.

IS IT OK FOR ME TO EXERCISE DURING MY JUICE FEAST?

Not only do I encourage it, I want you to get as much daily exercise as you can work in. I'm not talking about marathon running here! If you can take a long power walk with a minimum of 5000 steps and work up to 10,000 every day it will make a world of difference. Buy an inexpensive pedometer to keep track of your daily steps. Moderate exercise will leave you feeling energized and lighter while helping to stifle cravings. Try to find someone to walk with you if you need some extra motivation.

WHAT HAPPENS IF I MAKE A JUICE AND I DON'T LIKE THE TASTE?

Toss it, compost it, or give to the dogs and start over. This is a juice feast so if you don't like it, don't eat it! The very last thing I want you to do is eat something you don't like.

DAY-BY-DAY COACHING

PREP DAY 1

Hopefully you have read the book and have begun to prepare your inner and outer space for this amazing solid food vacation. If not, today is a great day to start! Read (or reread) Section 3 where I walk you through this absolutely necessary process. Organizing your outer space and getting rid of things that are no longer useful will help you prepare for your journey to better health. Clean out your closets and your cupboards. Get all processed and boxed foods out of your house to avoid temptation. Donate it or give it to a neighbor. Whatever you do, just don't eat it! If fruits and vegetables are not part of your regular diet, I'd like you to start eating them today. Start with 3 servings of fresh raw fruits and at least one serving of raw vegetables. Make yourself a colorful salad to eat with lunch or dinner today. Eat slowly and savor the pure raw deliciousness. If you have a juicer, you may even want to start your day with half a quart of juice. Just be sure to remember the 1/4 Green Rule. **If you don't have a juicer yet, go out, get one, and put it on your counter.**

I want you to get at least one raw vegan meal into your body today. If that's a tall order for you right now then trying making two meals 50% raw vegan.

It is of vital importance that you do some type of exercise each and every day from here on out. Go to a gym, take an aerobics class, or pop a DVD into the DVD player. At the very least, take a 20 minute brisk walk. The important thing is to get your body moving!

One of my favorite quotes comes from the "Tao Te Ching" by the ancient Chinese philosopher, Lao Tzu: "A journey of a thousand miles begins under your feet." Today you will be taking a momentous first step.

I hope you are excited! Be assured that in 10 short days you will be reaping the sweet benefits of change!

PREP DAY 2

Hopefully you started or are about to start your day with a juice. Today I would like you to double, YES DOUBLE, your intake of fresh raw fruits and vegetables. If you ate any unhealthy foods yesterday, you should definitely stay away from them today. This is why it is so important to get the junk food out of sight and out of mind! I would also like you to try to make two of your meals completely raw vegan today. If this is a tall order, I understand. How about one completely raw and two at 50% raw? The important thing is to make as much of your food consumption as raw as you can.

Yesterday, we focused on preparing your outer space for your juice feast. Today, we are going to focus on your inner space.

Knowing what motivates you will help you set yourself up for success so we are going to make that your primary focus for today. Find your unique motivation and circulate that message into every cell in your body. Feel your cells come to life with new found gratitude and enthusiasm as you keep that message in the forefront of your day.

Think about what changes you can make right now that will improve your day. Let me ask you a question ... Are you breathing? Your skin and lungs do some automatic breathing but are you consciously participating in the act of bringing energizing and cleansing oxygen into your cells?

Take a breath with me. Inhale through your nose pushing the air down so deep that you feel it in your belly. Hold it for a moment before exhaling out through your mouth. This is a cleansing breath that will help you reduce tension in both your body and mind. Do it often and I promise you will feel amazing!

In Section 3 of my book I talk about the importance of meditation. Whether you choose prayer, sitting meditation, or a nature walk, find at least 15 minutes a day and take some reflective quiet time for yourself.

Envision yourself at your ideal weight, free of pain, stress, and worries enjoying your morning juice. See yourself happy, healthy, and whole. Now hold this in your mind as we continue our journey over the next 9 days.

I'd like you to begin a journal. Record everything you eat on its pages, paying specific attention to any changes you are feeling in your body and mind. Reflect upon your quiet time and jot down some notes. Do you feel calmer or peaceful? Are you feeling less affected by what is going on around you?

You can use the journal provided at the end of the book or use your own. What's important is that you start journaling and stick with it through your entire feasting journey.

Tomorrow is a going to be a big day as you will be going all raw!

PREP DAY 3

I hope you are feeling well rested and rejuvenated this morning. You are well on your way to feeling and looking better than you have in years! I want you to give yourself a great big hug!

I'd like you to take a moment and ask yourself the following questions and please be honest with yourself. How do you feel about your food consumption yesterday? Did you sneak in any junk food? Are you pleased with your progress or do you think you could've eaten more raw vegan foods? If so, no worries, that means you may be better prepared for today than you might've thought!

I hope you are ready because today you will be taking a really big step as you will go COMPLETELY RAW! Try juicing at least three times today. You can have your juices for meals or snacks. The important thing today is that you consume ALL raw foods. Have as much raw fruit and vegetables as you'd like in between juicing, but consume absolutely no animal products and no cooked foods. I cannot stress the importance of this vital step to preparing your body for this amazing journey you are about to take.

Check your supplies and make sure that you are prepared to get through the first few days of your feasting. Trips to the grocery store should initially be avoided to avoid those processed temptations. After that, you will be well on your way and ready to experiment. If you need advice as to what to juice, check out Section 3 of my book, *Let's Go Shopping!*

Please, Please, Please, continue to work on your mind and spirit as well as your body. Take time to meditate. Make sure to do a little self-pampering. I know it can be tough sometimes but I know that you can find at least 35 minutes to do something good for yourself each and every day! That's 15 minutes of meditation and 20 minutes of exercise. You may even find that you enjoy it so much that you give yourself an hour.

It is so important to stay focused now. Remember your unique motivation and keep that message circulating through every cell in your body. Continue to jot down your thoughts in your journal. I hope that every shed of self doubt is gone. YOU CAN DO THIS! You essentially already are!

FEASTING DAY 1

Here you are — well on your way to a whole new YOU!

Remember, the first few days can be difficult depending on your normal diet but once you've passed the hump, it will be smooth sailing right to the finish line. Remember, it is of vital importance that you DO NOT DEPRIVE YOURSELF! If you feel hungry, make yourself a juice. You are feasting and you can have as much as you want!

As you dive into all juice nothing but juice today, please review Section 4 of my book, which will help give you some ideas as to what to juice. After a few juicy meals you will have a better idea of what your taste buds like and you will be ready to be creative and experiment.

Now, it is possible that you'll experience minor discomfort such as a bloated belly or a mild headache, although it's more likely that you will feel great! Remember, you are giving a deep cleaning to your entire digestive tract as well as all of your cells. You are literally feeling your body rid itself of toxins and any discomfort is a result of this process. The best way to let discomforts pass is to drink lots of water to help flush things through and to take it easy.

One thing that is likely to happen is that your mind may try to focus on food. The best thing you can do is distract it. Keep busy and productive and the time will pass quickly. Definitely do not stay home from work this week, as work will be a much needed distraction.

Review Section 3 of my book again and be sure that you are addressing your own personal needs. Being kind to yourself will certainly minimize discomfort as well. Get some meditation time into your day. Do a little pampering. And make sure that you move your body.

FEASTING DAY 2

You made it through the first day and I am so proud of you. The first step in your journey is always the hardest but every step is a step forward. I want you to focus on making PROGRESS one step at a time and before you know it, you will be the end of your juicy journey.

I bet you are already seeing and feeling the effects of your juice feasting excursion. You may notice that your body feels a bit lighter and your head feels clearer. Maybe you are already noticing some changes in your mirror. I bet you are less bloated. You may notice that your skin is brighter and clearer! Your eyes are probably less puffy and those dark circles are gone. Well, this is only the beginning! Imagine how great you will feel in another 5 days!

Now, I want you to ask yourself a question and I want you to remember that this is about YOU and not about me. Did you cheat? If you did, that's okay. It happens. Don't beat yourself up about it. The important thing is move on, get past it, and get back on track.

Here's a hint to help you avoid temptation. When the urge to cheat hits, walk outside and take 10 deep breaths or go for a brisk walk.

Call a supportive friend and get yourself a boost of moral support! Focus on all things positive and acknowledge your progress. Then go drink a tall glass of water or coconut water or make a juice!

Now, suck in that tummy, tighten those buttocks, fire up the juicer and strut your stuff! You can do this! You already are!

FEASTING DAY 3

Yes! You are really here at Day 3 where you are fast approaching hump day! I bet that you are feeling like a fog has lifted and that you feel super energized with a general feeling of lightness in your entire body! It really is amazing that it's only been 2 days and you are already starting to feel the positive changes in your body, isn't it?

Day 3 is a great day to start experimenting with your juicy concoctions. You've probably got an idea as to what you like best by now, whether it's a mix of leafy greens with something sweet or a spicy vegetable juice. One of my favorite green juices is kale, spinach, and lettuce juiced with pineapple! Try it — I bet you'll like it!

I'd like to remind you just how important it is to be moving your body. Fitness is an integral part of overall balance and health. The human body is designed to run and move and just like that exercise bike sitting in the basement, it will stiffen up if you don't use it. Exercising keeps blood, fluids, and vital energies flowing. Keeping up with your physical fitness will really help your body to purge all the nasty stuff.

Know that you can do it and let's keep moving forward one step at a time. You have come so far, perhaps farther than you thought you would. You've already done so much good for your body and you are more than halfway, so make it, make it, make it!

FEASTING DAY 4

Happy Hump Day! Here you are at Day 4 where you are now officially closer to the finish line than the starting point! There aren't many folks out there who will take the time to give themselves this juicy gift of health and wellness but you are doing it!

I want you to acknowledge this accomplishment and thank yourself and I want to encourage you to stick with it! I know it sounds crazy but Day 4 is a point where some folks drop off. Thoughts of solid and cooked foods enter the mind as they look forward to completing the feast and weakness strikes. Stick with it! Don't get distracted by the future, stay focused and stay in the present. This is the one and only body you will have in this lifetime, so give it the gift of health.

Don't worry if you've not been perfect. You are human and we humans are certainly not infallible! You are here to learn at a gradient that feels right for your body so remember that and just do it! Health is a process. You are giving yourself a strong foundation to continue building your own good health upon.

Remember your mantras. Keep your goals in the forefront of your mind. Stick with your journaling! Remember that you have made it over the hump and you can make it to the finish line! Just keep riding the wave and before you know it you will have reached your goals!

FEASTING DAY 5

Day 5 is upon us and I know you are starting to think about what happens next so I am going to give you a little information to put your mind to rest. But then you must get back to your feasting.

Some of you may be wondering if you can continue juicing. Yes, you absolutely can!

You may have even already decided to continue along your journey exploring a raw vegan diet. If you feel this is right for you, by all means please stick with it! If you haven't explored the pages of *ChefTinaJo.com*, please do so. My entire website is designed to help you transition to and maintain a healthy raw vegan diet. Be sure to check out my coaching programs if you are ready to go further in your journey!

If you took this vacation to rejuvenate and detox but wish to return to a standard American diet, you must do so with caution. Don't order a pizza on your first day back! You will begin by eating only raw fruits and vegetables on your first day back from your solid food vacation and remember to **drink lots of water**.

You will introduce cooked foods back into your diet gradually. Add some lightly steamed vegetables one day, then cooked whole grains such as brown rice and/or quinoa the next day. The important thing will be to listen to your body as you begin introducing cooked foods back into your diet. Your body will be very kind to you if at the very least you continue to drink a quart of fresh juice every morning so try to stay with that healthy new habit.

The bottom line is to be gentle coming off the feast. Too much too soon can create more damage than was done prior to feasting. You are doing an amazing job and you should be really proud of yourself for sticking with it.

FEASTING DAY 6

You are really looking great now. I bet that you are feeling vibrant and full of energy too! By now you should feel pretty much on top of the world. I hope you have been tracking your weight and noticing those pounds dropping! I bet your clothes are feeling a little loose! You may even need to reward yourself with some new ones!

You have taken some giant steps forward along this journey and you have been transformed because of it. I hope that you will take your new healthy habits and incorporate them into your daily routine. Taking time for yourself is just as important every day of your life as it is while you are vacationing.

A few more words about transitioning back to solid foods... My feasters often tell me that weaning off a feast was quite difficult. I think this is because people are afraid of returning to old and unhealthy habits.

This transition is the most important part of your feast. If you slip up here there's no turning back and you have just wasted your precious time!

Remember, the best thing to eat as you wean off your juicy feast is lots raw fruits with high water content; watermelons, grapefruit, grapes, apples, pineapples and melons for the first day.

You can go with light leafy blended soups, nut or seed milks (like sesame, almond or sunflower), or lightly steamed vegetables to prepare your system for heavier solids when and if you feel ready.

Regular blended (not juiced) fruit smoothies are another great option at this point. Stick to simple foods and you won't over-stimulate those digestive enzymes too soon.

Give yourself a great big hug and pat yourself on the back! You have just about reached your goals!

FEASTING DAY 7

CONGRATULATIONS!! Today is a very special day!!! Take a look at what you have just accomplished! These last 10 days were no small task but rather a huge milestone of accomplishment and you did it! I sincerely hope that you and the people in your life have noticed the changes in you.

My wish for you is that you continue along your journey to health and wellness. Regardless of how well or how poorly you did on this solid food vacation your journey has just begun and what an amazing journey lies ahead of you! Whether you continue your adventures in raw food or not is not as important to me as you discovering your own health potential. Find a healthy lifestyle that works for you and stick with it!

As I said yesterday, breaking off a feast can be just as hard, if not harder, than beginning one. I want to make sure you understand that. Follow my guidelines as presented in this book and you will be great!

Please take some time to reflect on your juicy experience as you transition back into your routine. Share your experience with friends and family. You have the ability to touch, inspire and improve the lives of those around you by sharing your story.

Please stop by from time to time and let us know how you are doing. You are a treasured member of our family and I hope you will stick around and maybe even try a few of my other programs or read another of my books.

And remember, "Health is not a state to aim for but a process to be continuously involved in."
— Paul Benson

Now go out into the world, strut your stuff and make some waves!

Here are a few simple, delicious juices to help get you started!

For more mouth watering recipes, be sure to visit my juice and smoothie tab on ChefTinaJo.com. Cheers!

CLEAN OUT THE REFRIGERATOR JUICE

Ingredients:

3 tomatoes

2 cucumbers

A hand full of cilantro

1 orange bell pepper

4 pieces of celery

1 Jalapeno pepper

OK perhaps the name is lacking, but it certainly gets the point across! I stood with the refrigerator door open waiting for something to call out JUICE ME and it did! My fridge needed tidying up and I needed some juice, so this was a win-win.

You should try it sometime. You'll be amazed with what you come up with! This was DELICIOUS!

THE AMAZING TRIO — CARROTS, CELERY AND GRAPES — OH MY!

Ingredients:

Carrot — 6 oz.

Celery — 6 oz.

Grape — 4 oz.

This amazing trio makes a fantastic juice combination! Not only is this juice truly tasty, but each ingredient has its own therapeutic strengths. Carrots and celery are both very alkalizing and cleansing to our bodies. Grapes, tiny but mighty, have been found to contain natural chemicals that have the potential to stop the spread of cancer cells. So DRINK UP!

You can now enjoy this delicious combination even more knowing its amazing healing benefits.

A WHOLE LOT OF LOVE

Ingredients:

Beet — 4 oz.

Wheatgrass — 2 oz.

Carrot — 5 oz.

Apple — 5 oz.

Beets are one of my favorite vegetables. They are sweet and oh so good for you. If you haven't tried them in juices before, you're in store for a treat. You'll be surprised at how much flavor these little guys carry. Beets are not only delicious, they are also very cleansing to the liver.

CABBAGE JUICE

Cabbage juice has some fantastic health benefits and has been used to treat conditions like constipation, colitis, hair loss and skin problems. It is also widely used to help heal ulcers.

I love cabbage juice straight with a squeeze of lime, but if you're new to cabbage juice try mixing it with 50% carrot or 50% apple juice then slowly work your way to full potency. Some folks can experience gas and cramps when drinking large amounts of cabbage juice. This can occur due to the cabbage reacting to the bacteria that exists in the intestines.

Ingredients

1 white or purple head of cabbage

Procedure

• Wash and remove any discolored outer leaves.

• Cut cabbage into 1/8 wedges or manageable size pieces for juicing. Then juice and enjoy!

GRAPE JUICE

If you have never had fresh homemade grape juice, I can assure you that you are missing out! It's nothing like store-bought juice. Freshly squeezed grape juice is more like nectar. It's thick, rich and smooth. I like to dilute mine with a bit of sparkling water for an extra special treat!

Ingredients

4 lbs grapes

Procedure

1. Wash and de-stem the grapes and place in a basin filled with water. Then rinse the individual grapes and place in another large bowl of clean water. Sort through the grapes, discarding the green unripe and old shriveled ones.

2. Run the grapes through your juicer. Dilute with sparkling water or purified drinking water, then enjoy!

KIWI, APPLE AND LIME JUICE

This juice is not only delicious, but it's high in Vitamin C and potassium and also rich in fiber. Kiwis pack a punch and they also make a gentle and effective laxative.

Ingredients

5 oz apple juice

9 oz kiwi juice

2 oz lime juice

Procedure

• Wash the apples and limes and peel the kiwi before juicing.

• Run all the ingredients through your juicer.

LOVE POTION NUMBER 5

I call this Love Potion Number 5 because I love all things beet and there are 5 ingredients to this juice. Simple enough, you say, but what is amazing about this combination of flavors is they are packed full of nutrients that will be surging through your body in the most delightful way.

Beets house amazing nutrients that are beneficial to our health. They are low in fat and contain Vitamins A, C, B1, B2 and B6 and the amount of antioxidants these beauties hold is off the charts! So experiment with beets and come up with your own love potion!

Ingredients

3 oz cabbage juice

3 oz celery juice

6 oz beet juice

1 oz lime juice

3 oz Swiss chard juice

Procedure

• Thoroughly wash all of your produce. Cut beets and cabbage into quarters for easier juicing. Depending on the size mouth of your juicer, you may also want to cut the lime in half.

• Run your ingredients through your juicer.

POMEGRANATE JUICE ELIXIR

Fresh is always best and you can make your own pomegranate juice at home. Pomegranates are full of antioxidants and nutrients with amazing anti-cancer properties. They also contain compounds that are good for your bones, brain, heart, lungs and teeth.

Ingredients

3–4 large Pomegranates (Typically 1/2 cup of juice is extracted from 1 pomegranate.)

Procedure

• Put on an apron or some protective clothing as this reddish purple juice can stain your clothing and the juicing process can be a bit messy; but it's well worth the effort!

• Cover your countertops with paper shopping bags or old dish towels to prevent staining.

• To remove the seeds: hold the pomegranate in your hand and use a heavy wooden spoon or other kitchen tool as a tapping device on the pomegranate. The idea is to completely tap the entire fruit so you loosen the seeds before opening.

• Peel the pomegranate skin off in 4 sections one at a time and peel open each section separately with your knife. Be careful not to cut completely through the fruit because this will cause you to lose precious juice and seeds.

• Hold the peeled pomegranate section over a large glass bowl (be careful not to use plastic, it will stain) and pull out the seeds using your fingers. Allow the seeds to fall into the bowl. The seeds are in pods throughout the pomegranate, so for our purposes here don't worry too much about removing every piece of the white pod as your milk bag will catch those pieces.   Another way to remove the seeds is to peel the entire pomegranate and submerge it into a bowl full of water. The water does help to release the seeds, but it also reduces the seeds' flavor by allowing some of the pomegranate juice to escape through this process. So if you use this method use a small amount of water.

• Once you've removed the seeds, add your bowl's contents to your food processor. Place the processor on pulse for a minute or two just to break up the seeds so they release their juice.

• Pour the blended pomegranate seeds into your milk bag over a clean bowl and squeeze the juice from the seed pulp. The seed fibers will remain in the milk bag. Continue to squeeze until no juice remains.

• You can enjoy the juice straight up or mix the pomegranate juice with orange, apple, grape juice or any other juice you desire. Pure pomegranate juice can taste a bit bitter; add a small amount of agave nectar to sweeten it to taste, if desired.

• Store remaining pomegranate juice in a glass container and refrigerate.

VIRGIN FUZZY NAVEL

Here's a fun bit of trivia. The Fuzzy Navel was one of the first drinks to arise in the new popularity of cocktails and mixed drinks in the 1980s. "Fuzzy" in the name refers to the peach and "navel" to the orange.

Peaches have a laxative and a powerful diuretic effect. They are comprised of more than 80 percent water and are a good source of dietary fiber, making them beneficial for those trying to lose weight.

Ingredients

2 cups freshly squeezed orange juice

5 whole peaches, pitted and sliced to fit juicer opening

1 whole lemon

Procedure

1. Juice your oranges then set aside while preparing peaches.

2. Thoroughly wash the peaches in cool water. Halve the peaches on a clean cutting board and remove the pits. Cut into slices that fit juicer.

3. Put the peaches into the juicer. Juice the lemon next. Add this mixture to the orange juice and then taste the juice. If the juice is too thick, you can add ice or more orange juice.

WATERMELON JUICE

Nothing cools me down faster on a hot summer's day than a fresh glass of watermelon juice.

If you've never tried watermelon juice before, you're in for a pleasant surprise; it's absolutely delicious! Watermelon is loaded with minerals, such as phosphorous, magnesium, and calcium. It's also particularly rich in potassium, which plays a key role in lowering blood pressure.

Ingredients

1 3lb watermelon

Procedure

1. If you're new to watermelon juice, I suggest you remove most of the rind and juice only a small section of it at first as it is has quite a bitter taste. Carefully slice the rind from the watermelon leaving as much of the pith as possible. This is the white layer between the fruit and the peel wherein lies a ton of vitamins and minerals that you don't want to miss out on!

2. Cut the watermelon into 1-2 inch manageable pieces and run through your juicer.

3. Run a handful of mint leaves through the juicer for a whole new amazing flavor dimension.

SMOOTHIE RECIPES

SMOOTHIE RECIPES

BERRY CRAZY SMOOTHIE WITH BEE POLLEN

Bee pollen is said to be one of nature's most completely nourishing foods. It has been called a true superfood. It is not only alkaline, but it is packed with proteins, enzymes and vitamins, including folic acid and B-complex. It has been referred to by health practitioners as an herbal fountain of youth as it is known to help increase energy and stamina, enhance sexuality, smooth wrinkles, help with weight loss, strengthen the immune system and even help prevent cancer.

Ingredients

1/2 cup frozen blueberries

1/2 cup strawberries (fresh, if available)

1/2 cup frozen raspberries

2 frozen bananas

1/2 cup pineapple

1 Tbsp bee pollen

1/2 cup water to desired thickness

Procedure

1. Place all ingredients in blender and blend till smooth and creamy.

BYE BYE BLACKBERRY SMOOTHIE

Berries are loaded with fiber. This helps you feel full (and eat less). They also top the charts in antioxidant power, protecting your body against free radicals and inflammation that are damaging to cells and organs. Simply put, eat more berries. Your body will thank you!

Ingredients

1 pint blackberries, frozen

1/4 cup blackberries, fresh

1/4 cup almonds

2 medjool dates

1 big handful spinach

1 cup filtered or alkaline water

Procedure

1. Blend all ingredients, EXCEPT the fresh blackberries, until smooth and creamy, adding water to desired consistency. Then top with blackberries for a deliciously filling drink.

SMOOTHIE RECIPES

CHERRY BANANA SMOOTHIE

This delicious treat is a refreshing breakfast or a pick-me-up any time of day. It's a great treat to get you on your feet and get you ready for the day or it can provide that extra boost to get you through to your next meal time.

Ingredients

2 cups frozen tart or organic sweet cherries

1 ripe banana, peeled (frozen is a great treat too)

1 cup almond milk

1 tsp psyllium powder (non-GMO)

Cherries, for garnish

Procedure

1. Put frozen cherries, banana and almond milk in blender and blend until smooth. If necessary, turn blender off, remove cover and scrape sides of container with a spatula. Continue to blend until smooth.

2. Pour into individual serving glasses. Garnish with cherries, if desired. Serve immediately.

SMOOTHIE RECIPES

EXOTIC SMOOTHIE

Mangosteen powder is a shining example of superfood purity and potency. Known as the "Queen of Fruits," mangosteen is a top antioxidant and anti-inflammatory agent containing an impressive array of vitamins, minerals, bioflavanoids and tannins. The addition of mangosteen powder makes this smoothie a real immune booster.

Ingredients

2 peaches

1 mango

1 banana

2 Tbsp mangosteen powder

Handful of ice

Water, as necessary

Procedure

1. Place all ingredients into blender and blend till smooth and creamy. Add water to desired consistency.

COCONUT MANGO LEMON BASIL MOJITO

Mangoes are high in iron making them great for pregnant women and people with anemia. They are also valuable in combating acidity and poor digestion. Mangoes contain phenols which have been shown to have a powerful antioxidant effect and anticancer abilities. So, what a better way to enjoy the benefits of this amazing fruit then this mojito?

Ingredients

9 cups coconut water

2 1/4 cups lime juice

1 cup agave nectar

9 cups frozen mango

3/4 cups fresh mango

1 1/4 cups basil leaves, chopped

1/2 tsp salt

1/3 cups powdered palm sugar

Procedure

1. Blend coconut water, lime juice, agave, frozen mango, fresh mango, and salt until smooth.

2. Pulse in basil lightly (too much will turn your smoothie green).

3. TO COAT GLASS: Fold a tea towel into a square and drench with water. Dip upside down martini or wine glass onto water soaked towel, and then lightly press into plate of palm sugar. This will ensure the palm sugar will stick to the glass.

4. Fill palm sugar-coated glass with beverage. Garnish with lemon wedges or slices and small basil leaves.

SMOOTHIE RECIPES

PAPAYA MINT SMOOTHIE

Papayas are not only delicious in taste, but they have a beautiful sunlit color. They are a rich source of antioxidants and nutrients, such as carotenes, Vitamin C and flavonoids. They contain a host of the B vitamins such as folate and pantothenic acid along with the minerals potassium and magnesium as well as a ton of fiber. All these nutrients help to promote the health of the cardiovascular system and also provide protection against colon cancer. In addition, the papaya is an amazingly rich source of the proteolytic enzymes which enable the digestion of protein. Papain; the most important of these enzymes, is found in the papaya.

Ingredients

Smoothie

4 cups frozen papaya

4 cups fresh papaya

4 cups orange juice

1 cup lime juice

1/4 cup agave nectar

6 leaves mint, chiffonade cut

2 cups coconut water

1 tsp palm sugar

12 cups shaved ice

Garnish

One mint leaf per glass

One slice of orange per glass

Procedure

1. Combine frozen and fresh papaya, orange juice, and lime juice in a high speed blender.

2. Blend till creamy.

3. Then add agave, coconut water, palm sugar, and mint.

4. Blend these until smooth and there are mint specs throughout.

5. Shred or shave the ice using the shredding blade of a food processor.

6. Place in freezer.

7. Using an ice cream scooper, place one or two scoops of ice in each glass.

8. Pour smoothie over ice, garnish, and serve immediately.

9. ENJOY!!!!!

Yield: 10 cups or approximately 5 servings. Cut as applicable to reduce yield.

CONCLUSION

You're obviously here right now because you know that you need to make some changes in your life. Change does not happen overnight but you will be pleasantly surprised how much you can change in just 7 short days. You have a chance to start turning your life and your health around right here, right now! Do you want a more positive outlook on every aspect of life? Are you ready to feel vibrant, alive and energized? Then stop what you're doing and ask...

When are you going to invest in YOURSELF? I'm hoping it's NOW!

Make Life Delicious,
Chef Tina Jo

JUICE FEAST JOURNAL

JUICE FEAST JOURNAL

_____

_____

_____

_____

_____

_____

_____

_____

_____

_____

_____

_____

_____

_____

_____

_____

_____

_____

_____

_____

_____

JUICE FEAST JOURNAL

JUICE FEAST JOURNAL

JUICE FEAST JOURNAL

_____

_____

_____

_____

_____

_____

_____

_____

_____

_____

_____

_____

_____

_____

_____

_____

_____

_____

_____

_____

JUICE FEAST JOURNAL

_____

_____

_____

_____

_____

_____

_____

_____

_____

_____

_____

_____

_____

_____

_____

_____

_____

_____

_____

_____

_____

_____

JUICE FEAST JOURNAL

JUICE FEAST JOURNAL

Chef Tina Jo began her raw vegan journey back in 1999 when a friend suggested a vegan detox program to help alleviate debilitating ovarian and uterine cysts. Having reached a dead end with conventional western medicine and desperate to find relief, Tina Jo attended her first detoxification program through Karyn Calabrese at Karyn's in Chicago, Illinois. That was the first step to a life changing experience.

"I'd tried everything — that is, every western drug and test available to womankind. It never occurred to me it could be my diet causing such havoc in my body!"

Tina Jo was so amazed at how good she felt after that first detox that she decided a raw diet was definitely worth pursuing. The change from the Standard American Diet to raw veganism not only cured her of the ovarian cysts and tumors, but seemed to be just what she needed to free herself from a history of emotional eating which had led to recurring bouts of anorexia and bulimia for a decade.

"I believe it was through the power of living foods that I learned to nourish my body, mind and spirit rather than just feeding emotions — finally allowing me to lay my food addictions to rest."

Chef Tina Jo knew in her heart that a diet of primarily raw vegan whole foods was right for her. Although she felt her best with a primarily raw diet, she would occasionally find herself slipping back into old familiar habits and her body let her know it didn't like it. "I'd feel a massive energy drop or get sick. When I was high to 100% raw, I felt and looked great! I knew the benefits of raw food — I lived it. So why couldn't I stick with raw?" It wasn't willpower, she realized, it was boredom! She needed to learn a new way to prepare meals. She needed to bring back the fun she used to have in the kitchen!! Chef Tina Jo literally grew up in the kitchen, as many Italian children do! "We did our homework, played games, did our hair, ate, cooked, and even bathed in the kitchen sink." Tina Jo grew to love that big old farm house sink. It was the best seat in the house to watch her mother prepare the family meal. "I was small and it was big, so we were a perfect match! In fact, I would beg my mother to put me in the sink where I would sit perched upon a pillow watching magic unfold in our kitchen."

Her mother was one of those cooks who never measured anything. She would just add a pinch of this and a handful of that tasting everything until it reached perfection. As Tina Jo grew too big for the sink she became her mother's assistant chef. "I was fascinated by the incredible meals she would create with no recipes. I would ask her how much salt or sugar to add and her response would always be, 'Just add until it tastes good.'" It was those fond childhood memories that eventually led Chef Tina Jo to the renowned Living Light Culinary Arts Institute in Ft. Bragg, California where she was able to merge her creative passion with a raw vegan diet. "I was so excited to bring fun back into the kitchen! Raw vegan does not have to be boring! Upon graduation I decided that I HAD to get this message out there!"

Chef Tina Jo

REAL LIFE RAW

Today, Chef Tina Jo is a highly respected Gourmet Raw Vegan Chef, Author, Speaker, and Coach known internationally for her humor and down-to-earth approach to raw veganism. Chef Tina Jo, along with her TV show Splendor in the Raw, has been awarded Top 10 Best Show, Best Chef, and Best Website in the Best of Raw 2009 Awards. She was awarded Top 10 Best Gourmet Chef, Funniest Raw Chef, and Sexiest Raw Woman as well as moving up into the Top 6 for Simple Raw Chef and Best Show in The Best of Raw 2010 Competition. Chef Tina Jo has made it her life's mission to bring super delicious, fresh, simple, fun, affordable raw vegan food to the mainstream.

Please visit my website, ChefTinaJo.com, where you will find more information including recipes, tips and tricks, and coaching programs to help you and your family transition to more raw foods. Be sure to check out the kids section under the "Raw Lifestyle" tab and join our chat community to get acquainted with other parents just like you!